LEARNING TO PAY ATTENTION

A SHORT INTRODUCTION TO MEDITATION

QUINN PATH

Copyright © 2026 by Quinn Path

All rights reserved.

No part of this book may be reproduced in any form or by any electronic or mechanical means, including information storage and retrieval systems, without written permission from the author, except for brief quotations in reviews.

Published by Pana Mind Press

CONTENTS

Introduction: What This Book Is For	1
Chapter 1: Attention, Not Silence	4
Chapter 2: What Happens When You Sit Still	8
Chapter 3: Thinking Is Not the Problem	13
Chapter 4: One Breath	18
Chapter 5: Noticing Without Holding	22
Chapter 6: Returning	26
Chapter 7: One Minute While Standing	30
Chapter 8: Walking From One Room to Another	34
Chapter 9: The Pause Before Speaking	38
Chapter 10: When Nothing Is Happening	42
Chapter 11: Sitting for Three Minutes	48
Chapter 12: Sitting for Ten Minutes	53
Chapter 13: Practicing Without a Schedule	59
Closing Note: What Paying Attention Becomes	64
A Small Request	67

INTRODUCTION: WHAT THIS BOOK IS FOR

This book is for people who want to understand meditation before committing to it.

You don't need prior experience. You don't need a quiet mind. You don't need a routine, a cushion, or a belief system.

You only need the ability to notice what is happening.

Meditation is often presented as something abstract or difficult, something that requires a lot of discipline, perfect calm, or long stretches of sitting still. I am going to show you a different approach. I am going to show you that meditation is a simple, practical skill that you can learn in very small steps.

At its simplest, meditation is learning how attention works.

Your attention is already active. It moves on its own. It shifts from sound to thought, from sensation to memory, from what is in front of you to what isn't . Most of the time, this happens without you realizing it. Meditation begins when that movement becomes visible.

This book is designed to help you see that movement clearly, without strain or pressure.

What Meditation Is and isn't

Meditation isn't about silence. It isn't about stopping thoughts. It isn't about reaching some special or perfect state. Those are the side effects.

It is about noticing what your attention is doing, moment by moment.

Sometimes what you notice will feel calm. Sometimes it will feel restless. Sometimes it will be dull, foggy, or repetitive.

All of these are workable. None of them is a step backward.

The practice doesn't depend on creating a particular kind of experience. It depends on seeing whatever experience is already here, as clearly as you can, while it is happening.

Why the Practices Are Short

Most books on meditation ask for long periods of sitting, especially at the beginning. That can be intimidating and off-putting for beginners.

This book uses very short practices on purpose.

A single minute of clear noticing is enough to train attention. A minute is long enough to see how your attention moves and short enough to fit into daily life without much resistance.

There are some longer practices later on, but they are optional. Nothing in this book requires more than a few minutes at a time.

Consistency matters more than duration.

How to Use This Book

Learning to Pay Attention

You can read this book straight through, or you can move slowly and return to chapters whenever you like.

Each chapter introduces one idea and one short practice. You are invited to try the practice, but you don't need to repeat it perfectly or follow it on a strict schedule.

If you skip a practice, the book still works. If you forget what you read, the book still works.

The aim isn't mastery. The aim is familiarity.

A Note on Expectations

This book doesn't promise constant calm, sudden clarity, or dramatic insight.

What it offers is a way to notice what is already happening, with less confusion and less effort. Over time, that kind of noticing can change how you relate to your thoughts, your body, and your actions.

Those changes are usually gradual. They are often quiet and subtle.

This book begins at the smallest possible scale.

CHAPTER 1: ATTENTION, NOT SILENCE

A lot of people say meditation is about quieting your mind.

For a lot of us, that idea is stressful right from the start. You sit down and pay attention, but your mind doesn't get quiet. If anything, it gets louder. Thoughts pop up. Sounds are suddenly clear. You might feel fidgety or heavy.

That's when a lot of people think, This isn't working.

That conclusion comes from a misunderstanding.

Meditation isn't really about silence at all.

It's really about attention.

Silence may appear sometimes. When it does, it doesn't stay. When it doesn't appear, the practice continues in the same way.

What Attention Is Doing Right Now

Right now, your attention is already active.

It may be on these words.

It may drift to a sound in the room.

It may move to a thought about something else you need to do.

You don't have to make this movement happen. It's already going on.

Most of the time, your attention moves all on its own. It jumps from one thing to another and sweeps you along for the ride. Meditation really starts when you begin to notice that movement.

Noticing is the action.

You're not trying to keep your attention stuck in one place. You're just learning to see where it goes, moment by moment.

Why Silence Is the Wrong Target

If silence were the goal, meditation would only work under ideal conditions. There would need to be no noise, no thoughts, and no interruptions.

But daily life doesn't work like that.

Your mind is always making new thoughts. That's not a failure; it's just how minds work. If you try to force silence, you'll usually end up feeling tense, and your attention drifts away from what's actually happening.

The practice doesn't depend on having fewer thoughts.

It depends on noticing that thoughts are present.

A busy mind is totally workable as long as you see it clearly.

A quiet mind that goes unnoticed isn't useful.

Sitting Reveals What Was Already There

When people first sit still, they often say their mind suddenly got busy.

The mind itself doesn't really change.

What actually changes is that the usual external distractions are gone.

In daily life, your attention gets pulled by all kinds of things like tasks, screens, and movement. When those things drop away, it's much easier to notice what your attention is doing.

It's a bit like walking into a quiet room and finally hearing a sound that was there the whole time. The noise didn't suddenly start when you walked in; you just noticed it.

Meditation works the same way.

A One Minute Practice

You don't need a special posture.

You can sit in a chair.

You can stand.

You can remain exactly as you are.

Try this:

1. Pause for one minute.

2. Notice whatever is most obvious in your experience.

This might be a sound, a physical sensation, a thought, or a visual impression.

There is no correct choice.

If your attention shifts, notice the shift.

If you forget the exercise and remember later, notice the remembering.

Each instance of noticing is the practice.

What Counts as Practice

Practice isn't measured by how steady or calm attention feels.

Practice is measured by your level of attention at any given point.

Even brief moments of noticing count. One clear moment is enough to establish the skill.

Longer practices build on this later. They don't replace it.

What to Notice Today

At some point today, pause briefly and notice where your attention is.

Notice how it moves ahead of what you are doing.

Notice how it returns.

Notice how it rests when nothing demands it.

You don't need to comment on this or improve it.

Seeing it is enough.

Next Chapter

In the next chapter, we will look at what typically happens when you sit still for the first few times, and why none of those experiences require correction.

CHAPTER 2: WHAT HAPPENS WHEN YOU SIT STILL

When you sit still for the first time, a few things tend to happen.

The body becomes more noticeable.

Thoughts become more obvious.

Time may feel slower.

This doesn't mean anything is wrong. It simply means your attention is no longer being occupied by movement and tasks. With fewer external demands, attention turns inward, making it easier to notice what was already present.

Why the Mind Feels Busier

Many people say their mind feels more active when they begin meditating.

This doesn't mean the mind has become busier. It means there is less distraction pulling attention away from it.

In daily life, attention is constantly redirected by messages, screens, and decisions. Much of our thinking stays in the background because something else is always happening. When you sit still, those distractions fall away. Attention has fewer places to go, so mental activity becomes more noticeable.

At first, this can feel uncomfortable. Thoughts may seem louder, emotions may feel closer, and physical sensations that were usually ignored may stand out.

This is a normal part of the process.

Restlessness Is Information

Restlessness often appears early in practice.

You may feel the urge to shift position.

You may want to stop and do something else.

You may check the time more than once.

These urges aren't problems. They're signals.

They show how quickly your attention moves toward distractions and away from stillness. Noticing this is part of the practice.

You don't need to act on restlessness.

You don't need to suppress it.

You only need to notice that it is present.

Boredom and Dullness

Some people experience boredom instead of restlessness.

Nothing seems to happen. The mind feels flat or repetitive. Attention drifts without much interest.

This is also workable.

Boredom shows how much your attention expects to be stimulated. When there's nothing new, your mind reacts. Just noticing this is enough.

There is no need to create interest.

There is no need to force alertness.

Let the experience be simple.

Strong Thoughts and Emotions

At times, thoughts may carry more emotional weight when you sit still.

Memories may appear.

Concerns may repeat.

Emotional reactions may surface without a clear cause.

This doesn't mean meditation is causing problems. It means you're no longer avoiding certain thoughts or feelings.

The instruction remains the same.

Notice what appears.

Notice how attention responds.

You don't need to analyze the content. You don't need to resolve anything.

Noticing how your attention moves around these experiences is the practice.

A One Minute Sitting Practice

Choose a place where you can sit comfortably for one minute.

Learning to Pay Attention

You can sit in a chair or on the edge of a bed. Keep your posture simple.

Try this:

1. Sit still for one minute.

2. Let your attention rest on whatever stands out most.

This may be a sensation in the body, a sound, or a thought.

If attention shifts, notice the shift.

If discomfort appears, notice the reaction to it.

Don't try to fix anything.

The goal isn't to sit perfectly still.

The goal is to notice what happens when you do.

What This Practice Is Showing You

Sitting still reveals patterns.

You may notice how often attention jumps ahead.

You may notice how quickly it reacts to discomfort.

You may notice how rarely it rests without effort.

These observations aren't judgments. They're just information.

Meditation makes these patterns visible.

After You Stand Up

When the minute ends and you return to activity, notice what remains.

You may feel no change at all.

You may feel slightly more aware.

You may simply notice that the practice ended.

All of these outcomes are fine.

The effects of practice add up over time. They come from repeating it, not from doing it intensely.

Next Chapter

In the next chapter, we'll look more closely at thinking and why thoughts don't get in the way of meditation unless your attention gets caught up in them.

CHAPTER 3: THINKING IS NOT THE PROBLEM

A lot of us tend to think that thoughts get in the way of meditation.

You sit down, notice your mind wandering, and it's easy to feel like you're doing something wrong. Suddenly, meditation can start to feel like a battle with your own mind.

This struggle is unnecessary.

Thinking isn't actually a problem for meditation.

It's only when you get swept away by your thoughts that it gets tricky.

Thoughts as Events

Thoughts appear in the same way sounds and sensations do.

A sound arises.

A sensation arises.

A thought arises.

The difference isn't the thought itself. The difference is how attention deals with it.

When your attention chases after a thought, it can turn into a whole story. But if you just notice the thought, it stays as a simple event passing by.

Meditation isn't about stopping your thoughts. It's more about simply noticing them as they show up.

Getting Lost and Noticing

Here's something important to keep in mind.

Sometimes attention becomes absorbed in a thought. You may replay a conversation, plan the day, or imagine something that isn't present. During that time, the thought feels continuous and convincing.

Then, at some point, you notice what has happened.

That moment of noticing is the practice.

It doesn't matter how long attention was lost.

It doesn't matter what the thought was about.

The return of attention is what matters.

Why Trying to Control Thoughts Backfires

Many beginners try to manage their thinking.

They push thoughts away.

They replace them with better ones.

They judge certain thoughts as distractions.

Learning to Pay Attention

All this just adds more mental noise. Suddenly, you're focused on controlling things instead of just observing what's going on.

You might even end up feeling more tense and less clear than when you started.

Meditation isn't about controlling anything.

It's really just about recognizing what's happening.

So, when a thought pops up, simply notice it.

When attention follows it, notice that too.

That's it. Nothing extra needed.

The Gap Between Thoughts

Sometimes there is a brief pause between thoughts.

It may be very short.

It may be subtle.

A lot of people end up chasing after this pause, hoping to make it last longer. But that usually just adds more effort and pressure.

You don't need to go looking for the pause. It'll show up on its own when you're not getting in the way.

If you notice a pause, great.

If you miss it, that's perfectly okay too.

Both are part of how this whole thing works.

A One Minute Practice

You can do this practice sitting or standing.

Try this:

1. Pause for one minute.

2. Notice when a thought appears.

You don't have to name the thought or figure out what it means.

Notice when attention follows the thought.

Notice when attention returns.

If you get totally caught up in thinking and forget what you're doing for a while, no worries. Just notice the moment you remember to come back.

That's the magic—that noticing is the practice itself.

What This Changes Over Time

With repetition, a shift begins to occur.

Thoughts will still come up, but they start to feel lighter. You'll catch yourself more quickly, and the space between getting lost and noticing shrinks bit by bit.

This shift happens slowly and naturally. There's no way to force it —and you don't need to.

It all comes from getting familiar with the practice, not from trying harder.

Thinking During Daily Life

You can use this same approach in everyday life, not just when you're sitting quietly.

You may notice a thought while walking.

You may notice planning while washing dishes.

You may notice irritation while waiting.

Each noticing moment works in the same way.

You don't need total peace and quiet for any of this.

All you need is a bit of attention to notice where your mind is going.

Next Chapter

Next up, we'll talk about using the breath as an easy way to bring your attention back. You'll see how even just one breath is enough to get started.

CHAPTER 4: ONE BREATH

The breath is typically introduced at the beginning of meditation practice.

But this can be confusing! A lot of people think they need to control their breath, make it deeper, or use it in some special way. If that doesn't come easily, it's easy to feel like meditation must be hard or complicated.

The truth is, it's not complicated at all.

Here's why we use the breath: it's always right there with you, going on in the background whether you notice it or not.

Why the Breath Is Useful

The breath is great for three simple reasons:

It's always happening in the present moment.

It does its thing without you having to manage it.

And you can actually feel it happening, right now.

You don't have to picture the breath, fix it, or hold onto it in any special way.

Your attention can settle on the breath naturally, without any effort. It doesn't need a big explanation or anything fancy.

One Breath Is Enough

Many meditation guides will tell you to follow your breath continuously.

But you don't have to do it that way here.

You don't have to focus on your breath for minutes at a stretch.

You don't need to stick with it the whole time, either.

Even just noticing a single breath is enough.

Simply noticing one in-breath or out-breath is all it takes to get started. After that, your attention will wander—that's totally normal, and it's part of the process.

The Role of Returning

At some point, your mind is bound to wander away from your breath.

That's completely expected.

Coming back to the breath isn't about forcing your attention. It's just about noticing that your mind wandered, and letting it gently find its way back.

Think of the breath as a cozy spot your attention can return to whenever it wants—nothing more, nothing less.

There is no need to hurry.

Success isn't the goal; just participate in the practice.

That act of returning? That's the real skill you're building.

Letting the Breath Be Natural

Don't mess with your breathing.

No need to slow it down.

Don't try to make it deeper.

And don't stress about breathing the 'right' way.

Just let your breath do its own thing, however it shows up.

Let your attention follow your breath, just as it is—not how you think it should be.

A One Minute Practice

You can try this practice while sitting, standing, or however you feel comfortable.

Try this:

1. Pause whatever you're doing for just one minute.

2. Notice one complete breath.

Feel your in-breath or your out-breath, go with whichever feels easiest to notice.

When that breath is over, let your attention move wherever it wants to go.

If your attention drifts back to your breath, just notice another single breath.

If your mind wanders somewhere else, simply notice that, too.

There's no need to count breaths or keep track of anything.

Common Misunderstandings

If you forget about your breath, that's totally okay—nothing's gone wrong.

If your breath feels kind of faint or hard to notice, that's fine too.

If your attention keeps wandering, it's all good. That's just part of the experience.

The breath isn't some kind of test—it's just a gentle point of reference.

Using the Breath During the Day

You don't even have to sit down to do this practice.

You can notice one breath when you're waiting for something.

You can notice one breath while you're standing around.

You can even take a breath before you say something.

Every time, the steps are the same.

Just notice a single breath.

Let your attention move wherever it wants to after that.

And that's really all you need.

Next Chapter

Next, we'll look at how attention sometimes tries to hold onto experiences, and how just noticing them—without trying to hold on—lets things move more naturally.

CHAPTER 5: NOTICING WITHOUT HOLDING

When people first start paying attention, they often do one extra thing without realizing it.

They try to hold the experience in place.

A sensation appears, and they cling to it.

A moment of focus happens, and they try to keep it going.

A calm feeling comes over them, and they try not to lose it.

This is understandable, because it feels like progress.

But holding isn't the same as noticing.

What Holding Feels Like

Holding usually comes with effort.

You may notice yourself tightening slightly.

You may feel like you are watching too closely.

You may feel disappointed when the experience changes.

That disappointment is a clue.

It shows that attention has shifted from noticing what is happening to trying to prevent something from ending.

Experience is always changing. When attention tries to freeze it, it results in tension.

What Noticing Is Like

Noticing is simpler.

Something appears.

You are aware of it.

It changes or disappears.

Nothing more needs to be added.

When attention is simply noticing, experience moves naturally. Sounds fade, sensations shift, and thoughts pass by.

You don't need to help this process along.

A Common Example

Imagine listening to a sound, maybe a bird singing or a car driving by.

At first, you just hear it.

You might think, This is good; I'm paying attention.

When the sound fades, you might notice a small sense of loss.

That feeling isn't really about the sound itself. It's about wanting to hold on.

The practice isn't to keep the sound from ending.

The practice is to notice that the sound has changed.

Letting Experience Move

Experience doesn't need permission to move.

Attention sometimes tries to slow things down or keep them steady. This can be subtle.

When you notice yourself doing this, there's nothing to fix.

Just notice the holding.

Then notice what happens when you let go.

Usually, experience returns to its natural pace.

A One Minute Practice

You can do this practice sitting or standing.

Try this:

1. Pause for one minute.

2. Notice the most obvious sensation in your body.

It might be pressure, warmth, movement, or contact with the ground.

Notice it without trying to hold it in place.

When it changes, notice the change.

When something else becomes more obvious, notice that instead.

There is no need to stay with one thing.

When Attention Grips

Sometimes attention grips automatically.

You may catch yourself trying to focus harder.

You may feel slightly tense or impatient.

That is fine.

Noticing the grip is already a release.

You don't need to relax on purpose.

You don't need to correct anything.

Seeing the habit is enough.

Taking This Into the Day

You will notice holding throughout the day.

You may hold onto a thought.

You may hold onto a reaction.

You may hold onto a moment you liked.

Each time, notice the holding without judging yourself.

Then let attention move again.

Next Chapter

In the next chapter, we will talk about returning to the practice, what it really means, and why forgetting is actually part of learning.

CHAPTER 6: RETURNING

People often think meditation is about staying focused.

In practice, it is mostly about coming back.

Attention moves on its own. It drifts to sounds, thoughts, memories, plans. This isn't a mistake. It is what attention does.

The skill being developed isn't about preventing attention from moving. It is about noticing when it moves and returning.

What Returning Actually Means

Returning doesn't mean snapping attention back into place.

It doesn't mean forcing focus.

It doesn't mean doing something sharply or quickly.

Returning simply means noticing that attention has shifted and letting it settle again.

This recognition is the most important part of the practice.

You might notice you were thinking about something else.

You might notice you were distracted for a while.

You might notice you completely forgot the practice.

The moment you notice any of this, you have already returned.

Forgetting Is Part of the Process

Many people treat forgetting as failure.

They think the practice only counts if they remember it the whole time. This creates unnecessary pressure.

Forgetting is built into the practice.

If attention did not wander, there would be nothing to notice and nothing to return from. The movement away and the return are part of the same process.

Each time attention comes back, the skill is reinforced.

Returning Without Commentary

When you notice that attention has wandered, there is often an extra reaction.

You might judge yourself.

You might feel annoyed.

You might think you should be better at this.

These reactions are simply more experiences to notice.

You don't need to correct them or push them away. You also don't need to follow them.

Notice the wandering.

Notice the reaction.

Then allow attention to settle again.

Nothing else is required.

A Simple Example

Imagine reading a page and realizing you don't remember the last paragraph.

At the moment you realize this, attention has returned. You don't need to reread the page with frustration. You simply continue.

Meditation works the same way.

The return is quiet. It doesn't need emphasis.

A One Minute Practice

You can do this practice anywhere.

Try this:

1. Pause for one minute.

2. Let attention rest wherever it goes.

When you notice that attention has moved away from the present moment, acknowledge it.

Then allow attention to return naturally.

You don't need to decide where it returns to. You don't need to choose a focus point.

The noticing and the return happen together.

Returning During the Day

This skill applies outside of formal practice.

Learning to Pay Attention

You may notice that you have been lost in thought while walking.

You may notice that you reacted automatically in a conversation.

You may notice that your attention rushed ahead of what you were doing.

Each noticing moment is a return.

There is no need to stop what you are doing. Simply continue with a bit more awareness.

What Changes Over Time

With repetition, returning becomes more familiar.

Attention will still move, but you will notice it sooner. The time between wandering and noticing becomes shorter, and returning feels less like effort and more like a gentle reset.

This change happens gradually.

You don't need to track it.

Next Chapter

In the next chapter, we will move on from sitting and explore how practice can continue while standing, using the body as a clear reference point.

CHAPTER 7: ONE MINUTE WHILE STANDING

Meditation doesn't require sitting down.

You don't need a quiet room or a specific posture. You don't need to close your eyes or step away from what you are doing.

You can practice while standing.

Standing is helpful because it is a regular part of life. You stand many times each day, often without paying much attention.

Why Standing Works

When you stand, the body gives you clear information.

You can feel your weight.

You can feel pressure through your feet.

You can feel small adjustments as balance shifts.

These sensations are steady enough to notice, but not so strong that they demand your attention. This makes them a good reference point for practice.

The focus isn't on improving the body. The practice is about noticing what is already happening.

No Need to Freeze

Standing practice doesn't mean standing stiffly.

You can stand naturally.

You can sway slightly.

You can adjust your posture if needed.

The practice isn't about staying completely still. It is about noticing how standing feels as it changes from moment to moment.

A One Minute Standing Practice

You can do this anywhere you are already standing.

Try this:

1. Stand for one minute.

2. Notice the contact between your feet and the ground.

Feel the pressure.

Notice how the weight shifts without effort.

If attention moves to a thought or a sound, notice that. Then notice the feeling of standing again.

You don't need to keep your focus on your feet the entire time. Allow attention to move naturally.

What You Might Notice

You may notice tension in your legs or back.

You may notice subtle movement.

You may notice impatience or the urge to move.

All of this is fine.

The aim isn't comfort or complete stillness. The aim is to observe how attention connects with the body while standing.

Standing in Daily Life

This practice fits easily into ordinary moments.

You can try it while waiting for the kettle.

You can try it in a line.

You can try it before leaving a room.

There is no need to let others know you are practicing. You are simply noticing the experience of standing.

One minute is enough.

When Attention Drifts

As with every practice in this book, attention will drift.

You might forget what you were doing.

You might get pulled into planning or reacting.

When you notice this, the practice is already happening.

Notice the drifting.

Notice the return to standing.

Nothing else is required.

Why This Matters

Practicing while standing shows you something important.

Meditation doesn't require a special setup. It can happen during ordinary activities. Attention doesn't need perfect conditions to be noticed.

Standing practice makes this obvious.

Next Chapter

In the next chapter, we will explore how walking from one room to another can turn transitions into natural opportunities for practice.

CHAPTER 8: WALKING FROM ONE ROOM TO ANOTHER

Most walking happens on autopilot.

You stand up. You move. You arrive somewhere else. Attention is usually already ahead of the body, thinking about what comes next.

This makes walking an ideal place to practice.

There is no need to walk slowly or change how you walk. Simply notice that you are walking.

Why Transitions Matter

Transitions are the moments between tasks.

Leaving one room.

Entering another.

Moving from sitting to standing.

Attention often rushes through transitions and jumps ahead to what comes next.

Noticing a transition interrupts that habit in a very simple way.

This isn't about adding a new activity. It is about paying attention to something that is already part of your day.

Walking Without Adjusting

This isn't a walking technique.

You don't need to slow down.

You don't need to match your steps to your breath.

You don't need to hold your posture in a certain way.

Walk as you normally do.

The goal of the practice is to notice movement, not to change or improve it.

A One Minute Walking Practice

Choose a short distance, like walking from one room to another.

Try this:

1. Begin walking as you normally would.

2. Notice the feeling of movement.

Feel the shift of weight.

Feel the contact of your feet with the floor.

Notice the rhythm of stepping.

If your attention shifts to a thought or a sound, simply notice that, and then return your focus to walking.

There is no need to stay with one sensation.

. . .

Arriving Without Rushing

When you arrive at your destination, pause briefly.

Notice that the walking has ended.

Notice the change in posture.

There is no need to stop moving completely. Just let yourself notice that you have arrived.

This pause can be very short.

Common Reactions

You may feel that this practice is too simple.

You may forget to do it halfway through.

You may remember only after you arrive.

All of these reactions are normal.

If you remember at any point, the practice is working.

Using Walking Throughout the Day

You walk many times each day without planning to practice.

Each transition is an opportunity.

You can notice walking:
- when leaving the bathroom,
- when going to the kitchen,
- when moving between rooms.

There is no need for any special setup.

· · ·

What This Teaches

Walking practice shows how often attention precedes the body.

It also shows that attention can return to the present moment without much effort.

By noticing walking, even briefly, you train your attention to stay closer to what is actually happening.

Next Chapter

In the next chapter, we will explore the pause before speaking and how attention can influence the moment just before action.

CHAPTER 9: THE PAUSE BEFORE SPEAKING

Most speech happens quickly.

Something is said.

A reaction appears.

Words come out.

Often, attention arrives after the sentence has already started.

This chapter is about noticing the brief moment just before speaking.

What Happens Before Words

Before you speak, there is usually a small buildup.

You may feel an urge to respond.

You may feel tension in the body.

You may feel the need to explain, defend, or correct something.

This buildup often happens very fast. It is easy to miss.

The practice isn't about stopping yourself from speaking. The intention is to notice the buildup that happens before you speak.

The Pause Is Very Small

The pause before speaking isn't a long gap.

It may last less than a second.

It may feel more like a shift than a pause.

That is enough.

You don't need to slow down conversations or become quiet or withdrawn.

You are only noticing what happens right before the action.

Why This Matters

Speech is one of the clearest places where habits show up.

The same reactions tend to repeat.

The same phrases appear.

The same tones come out.

By noticing the moment before speaking, attention begins to see these patterns in real time.

Nothing needs to change immediately.

Seeing the pattern is the work.

A Simple Example

Someone says something you disagree with.

A response forms quickly.

You feel ready to speak.

If you notice that sense of readiness, even for a moment, you are practicing.

You may still say the same words.

You may say something different.

Either way, your attention has become involved earlier than it normally would.

A One Minute Practice

You don't need a formal setup for this.

Try this:

1. During a conversation, notice the moment before you speak.

2. See if you can feel the urge or movement toward speech.

You don't need to hold back.

You don't need to pause dramatically.

Just notice that the urge is there.

If you forget to notice until after you have spoken, that still counts as part of the practice.

After the Words Are Out

Sometimes you will only notice after you have spoken.

You may realize that you reacted automatically.

You may realize that attention was not present.

This is completely normal.

Notice the recognition.

Notice how attention comes back after the fact.

That return of attention is part of the same process.

Taking This Lightly

This practice isn't about becoming careful or controlled.

If you try to monitor everything you say, you'll feel tension.

Keep this light.

You are not watching yourself from a distance. You are simply noticing when your attention arrives a bit earlier than usual.

Using This Outside Conversation

The same pause appears before other actions.

Before sending a message.

Before clicking a link.

Before reacting internally.

Each time you notice that moment, you are learning how to arrive sooner.

Next Chapter

In the next chapter, we will explore what it feels like when practice seems uneventful, flat, or unclear, and why those moments are not a problem.

CHAPTER 10: WHEN NOTHING IS HAPPENING

At some point, many people reach a quiet conclusion.

Nothing is happening.

They have been trying the practices. They have been noticing their breath, their body, their movement through the day. They have been pausing here and there.

And it feels flat.

No insight.

No calm.

No obvious change.

This chapter is about that moment.

The Expectation of Something

Most people come to meditation with an expectation, even if they are not aware of it.

They expect a feeling.

They expect a shift.

They expect something to arrive.

When nothing noticeable arrives, disappointment follows.

That disappointment isn't a sign that the practice is failing. It is a sign that attention is still waiting for a result.

Seeing that waiting is part of the practice.

Why Nothing Feels Uncomfortable

Doing nothing is harder than it sounds.

When there is no strong sensation, no emotional charge, and no clear focus, attention becomes restless. It looks for something to latch onto.

This can feel dull or pointless.

But what you are noticing in these moments isn't emptiness. You are noticing the habit of seeking stimulation.

That habit is usually hidden by constant activity.

Nothing Is Still an Experience

It is easy to overlook this, but nothing happening is still something happening.

There may be a quiet background sense of being present.

There may be a soft awareness of the body.

There may be simple alertness without a clear object.

These experiences are subtle. They don't announce themselves.

Because they are not dramatic, they are often dismissed.

But learning to notice what is subtle is one of the skills meditation develops.

The Urge to Improve

When nothing seems to be happening, another impulse often appears.

The urge to improve the practice.

You might try to focus harder.

You might change techniques.

You might decide you are not doing it right.

This urge makes sense. It comes from wanting reassurance.

But improvement isn't the goal here.

The practice isn't about making something happen. It is about seeing what is already happening, including the urge to change things.

A Familiar Everyday Example

Think about waiting in line with nothing to do.

No phone.

No conversation.

No distraction.

At first, it feels uncomfortable. Time stretches. You become aware of your posture, your breathing, your impatience.

Learning to Pay Attention

Eventually, something shifts. You stop fighting the waiting.

Meditation works in a similar way.

Nothing happening is often the doorway into noticing more quietly.

A One Minute Practice

This practice may feel strange at first.

Try this:

1. Pause for one minute.

2.. Don't choose anything specific to focus on.

Let attention rest wherever it naturally settles.

If nothing stands out, notice that.

If you feel bored or impatient, notice that.

If you feel calm, notice that too.

There isn't hing to correct.

The point is to see what attention does when it isn't being directed.

When You Want to Stop

Sometimes the strongest reaction to nothing happening is the desire to quit.

This can show up as:

This is pointless.

I am wasting my time.

I should be doing something else.

These thoughts are not a problem.

Notice them the same way you notice anything else.

Notice the pull to leave.

Notice what attention does with that pull.

You don't need to stay longer. You only need to notice what is happening right now.

Trusting the Quiet Work

The effects of meditation often show up indirectly.

You may notice reactions sooner.

You may notice pauses where there were none before.

You may find yourself less caught by certain habits.

These changes don't come from dramatic moments. They come from repeated, uneventful noticing.

Nothing happening isn't a dead end.

It is where attention learns to stop chasing.

Taking This Forward

When practice feels flat, simple, or unremarkable, that doesn't mean it has stopped working.

It means attention isn't being entertained anymore.

That isn't something to fix.

It's something to recognize.

. . .

Next Chapter

In the next chapter, we will return to sitting, starting with a short three-minute sit, and look at how stillness works when nothing else is competing for attention.

CHAPTER 11: SITTING FOR THREE MINUTES

Up to this point, most of the practices in this book have fit easily into movement.

Standing.

Walking.

Pausing briefly during the day.

Sitting changes the situation.

When you sit down and stop moving, your attention has fewer places to go. This makes patterns easier to see.

That is why sitting is useful, even in very short amounts.

Why Three Minutes Is Enough

Three minutes doesn't sound like much.

That is exactly the point.

Long sits can feel heavy before they feel helpful. They invite expectations, resistance, and planning. Three minutes avoids most of that.

It is short enough that you can begin without negotiation. It is long enough for attention to show its habits.

You are not trying to settle into a state.

You are giving attention to a small window to reveal itself.

Keep the Setup Ordinary

You don't need a special place.

Sit in a chair.

Sit on the edge of a bed.

Sit somewhere you already are.

Let your feet rest on the floor if that feels natural. Let your hands rest where they fall.

The goal isn't posture. The goal is staying put for a few minutes without turning the sit into a project.

What You Are Actually Doing

During the sit, you are doing the same thing you have been doing throughout the book.

You are noticing where attention goes.

Sometimes it will rest on the breath.

Sometimes it will move to sound.

Sometimes it will drift into thought.

There is no correct object to focus on.

If attention is present and visible at any point, the practice is happening.

A Three-Minute Sitting Practice

Set a timer for three minutes.

Try this:

1. Sit and allow your body to settle.

2. Notice whatever stands out in your experience.

This might be a sensation in the body, the feeling of breathing, a sound, or a thought.

If attention moves, notice the movement.

If you forget the practice and remember later, notice the remembering.

There's no need to restart. There's no need to correct anything.

When the Body Wants to Move

Discomfort often appears when sitting.

An itch.

A shift in posture.

The urge to adjust.

You don't need to stay perfectly still.

If you move, notice the decision to move.

If you stay still, notice the urge.

Both responses are part of the same pattern.

. . .

When the Mind Wanders

It is very common to lose track of the sit.

You may realize near the end that you have been thinking for most of the time. That realization isn't a failure.

It is the practice.

The moment attention notices itself again is the moment that matters.

Ending the Sit

When the timer ends, notice the ending.

Notice the impulse to get up or move on.

Notice how attention shifts toward the next activity.

Then stand up and continue with your day.

There's no need to reflect on or evaluate the situation.

How Often to Do This

You don't need to sit every day.

You can use a three-minute sit to check in with your attention more clearly. You can also skip it entirely and rely on everyday practices.

This sit is a tool, not a requirement.

Why Short Sitting Works

Short sitting works because it lowers the stakes.

You are not trying to improve yourself.

You are not training endurance.

You are giving attention to a brief, quiet space to show how it behaves when nothing else is competing for it.

Three minutes is enough for that.

Next Chapter

In the next chapter, we will extend this to a longer sit, looking at what changes, what stays the same, and what beginners often misunderstand when they sit for ten minutes.

CHAPTER 12: SITTING FOR TEN MINUTES

At some point, many people wonder whether they should sit longer.

Three minutes felt manageable.

It showed you something.

Now the question appears naturally.

What happens if I sit for longer?

This chapter answers that question without turning sitting into a test.

Why Ten Minutes Is Different

Ten minutes isn't a dramatic increase, but it changes the experience.

In the first few minutes, attention is still settling.

By the middle, habits become clearer.

Toward the end, there is often a shift in how time feels.

This doesn't mean anything special is supposed to happen. It means attention has fewer ways to escape.

Ten minutes gives patterns enough time to repeat.

What Usually Happens

Most ten-minute sits include a mix of experiences.

You may feel focused for a short while.

You may feel distracted for a while longer.

You may forget you are sitting at all.

None of this is unusual.

The mistake is thinking the sit should feel steady or calm from start to finish. That expectation creates unnecessary effort.

The sit isn't a performance. It is a sample.

The Middle Is Often the Hardest

Many people find the middle of a ten-minute sit uncomfortable.

The beginning feels purposeful.

The end feels close.

The middle feels exposed.

This is where boredom, restlessness, or doubt often appear.

You might think:

Why am I doing this?

This isn't working.

I should stop.

These thoughts are not interruptions. They are part of the pattern the sit reveals.

Noticing them is the practice.

You Are Still Doing the Same Thing

It is important to be clear about this.

A ten-minute sit doesn't add a new technique.

You are still noticing where attention goes.

You are still noticing when it moves.

You are still noticing when it returns.

Nothing else changes.

If attention rests on the breath for a while, fine.

If it moves to sounds or thoughts, also fine.

You don't need to choose correctly.

A Ten-Minute Sitting Practice

If you decide to try this, keep the setup simple.

Sit comfortably.

Set a timer for ten minutes.

Try this:

1. Sit and let attention settle wherever it goes.

2. Notice movement, distraction, and return.

You don't need to stay with one object.

You don't need to improve the sit as it goes on.

If you spend most of the time lost in thought and only notice near the end, that noticing still counts.

When Discomfort Appears

Ten minutes gives discomfort more time to show up.

You may feel stiffness.

You may want to adjust.

You may feel impatient.

You don't need to endure discomfort to benefit from the sit.

If you move, notice the decision to move.

If you stay still, notice the urge to move.

Either way, attention is learning.

When Nothing Seems to Happen

Some sits feel uneventful.

No strong thoughts.

No clear focus.

No obvious insight.

These sits can feel pointless.

They are not.

Learning to Pay Attention

They show how much attention is expected for something to occur. Seeing that expectation is part of the practice.

After the Sit Ends

When the timer ends, notice what happens next.

You may feel relief.

You may feel disappointed.

You may feel nothing at all.

Don't evaluate the sit.

Simply stand up and continue your day.

The effect of longer sitting shows up gradually, often outside the sit itself.

How Often to Sit This Long

You don't need to sit for ten minutes every day.

You can use this practice occasionally to deepen your familiarity with attention.

Three-minute sits, and everyday practices still do most of the work.

Longer sits support them. They don't replace them.

Why Longer Sitting Helps

Longer sitting makes attention easier to recognize.

With time, you may notice that attention returns more quickly, even outside formal practice. This isn't something you need to aim for. It happens naturally as familiarity grows.

Ten minutes is simply one way to allow that familiarity to develop.

Next Chapter

In the next chapter, we will look at how practice fits into real life without schedules, streaks, or plans, and how attention becomes something you carry rather than something you set aside time for.

CHAPTER 13: PRACTICING WITHOUT A SCHEDULE

Many people assume meditation only works if it is done regularly, at the same time, in the same way.

They think in terms of routines, streaks, or plans.

This chapter takes a different approach.

The practices in this book are meant to fit into life as it is, not life as it looks on a schedule.

Why Schedules Often Fail

Schedules work well for tasks that have clear beginnings and endings.

Meditation is different.

Attention doesn't turn on at a specific time. It moves continuously throughout the day. Trying to confine practice to a fixed slot can make it feel separate from the rest of life.

When a schedule breaks, practice often disappears with it.

This doesn't mean the intention was weak. It means the structure was too rigid.

What Practice Actually Depends On

Practice depends on noticing.

It doesn't depend on:

- the time of day,
- the length of the session,
- or how many days in a row you have practiced.

If attention becomes visible, even briefly, practice is happening.

This can occur while sitting, walking, speaking, or waiting.

The form matters less than the recognition.

Letting Practice Be Opportunistic

Instead of planning practice, let it happen when conditions allow.

You may notice attention while standing in the kitchen.

You may notice it as you walk to another room.

You may notice it in the middle of a conversation.

These moments don't need to be marked or counted.

They are complete on their own.

Over time, attention learns to arrive more often simply because it has been noticed repeatedly.

Using Sitting When It Makes Sense

Sitting still can be useful, but it doesn't need to be frequent or fixed.

You might sit:

- when you feel scattered,
- when you are curious,
- or when you have a few quiet minutes.

Three minutes is enough. Ten minutes is optional.

Sitting supports everyday practice. It doesn't replace it.

When Practice Feels Inconsistent

There will be days when you forget completely.

There will be stretches when practice feels distant.

This doesn't undo anything.

Attention doesn't lose its capacity to notice. It simply waits until conditions allow recognition again.

When noticing returns, practice resumes immediately.

There's no need to restart or catch up.

Dropping the Idea of Progress

It is tempting to measure meditation.

Am I calmer?

Am I better at this?

Is it working?

These questions pull attention away from what is happening now.

Progress in this kind of practice is indirect. It shows up as familiarity, not achievement.

You may notice reactions sooner.

You may recover more quickly.

You may pause where you did not before.

These changes are easiest to see after the fact.

Keeping It Simple

If practice starts to feel heavy, simplify.

Return to one breath.

Return to standing.

Return to noticing for one minute.

There's no advanced version of this practice. There's only repetition with less effort.

Letting Practice Fade and Return

Practice doesn't need to be constant to be effective.

It can fade for a while and return later.

What matters is noticing attention, without making it into a task.

That recognition is enough.

A Short Reminder

You don't need a routine to practice.

You don't need to be consistent.

You don't need to do this every day.

You only need to notice when attention is present.

Everything else is optional.

Closing Note

In the final section, we will look at what this way of paying attention becomes over time, and how it settles quietly into daily life without effort or expectation.

CLOSING NOTE: WHAT PAYING ATTENTION BECOMES

At some point, the practices in this book stop feeling like practices.

You notice attention without trying to.

You pause without planning to.

You recognize movement without naming it.

Nothing dramatic announces this shift. It happens quietly, over time.

This isn't about achievement. It's about familiarity.

Attention as Something Ordinary

Attention doesn't need to be trained into something special.

It already knows how to notice.

It already knows how to return.

What changes is how often this is seen.

As attention becomes more familiar, it takes up less space. You stop checking whether you are doing it correctly. You stop waiting for a result.

Paying attention becomes part of how you move through the day.

No Final Instruction

There is no final technique to add.

You don't need to refine anything.

You don't need to deepen the practice.

You don't need to keep improving.

If you notice attention moving, the practice is present.

If you don't notice it for a while, nothing is lost.

How This Continues

You may continue sitting occasionally.

You may rely mostly on everyday moments.

You may forget about meditation entirely for stretches of time.

All of this is fine.

The capacity to notice doesn't disappear. It remains available whenever conditions allow it to show up again.

When Doubt Appears

You may wonder whether this is enough.

Whether you should be doing more.

Whether something deeper is missing.

These thoughts are also part of experience.

You can notice them in the same way you notice anything else.

Letting This Be Small

This book has stayed small on purpose.

Short practices.

Ordinary settings.

Minimal instruction.

This isn't a limitation. It is the point.

Paying attention doesn't need to be built up. It needs to be recognized.

A Final Reminder

If you take nothing else from this book, take this.

You don't need to set aside time to pay attention.

You don't need to wait for the right conditions.

Attention is already active.

Noticing that, even briefly, is enough.

A SMALL REQUEST

If this book was helpful for you, you might consider leaving a short review wherever you picked it up.

Reviews make a real difference for quiet books like this. They help other readers gauge whether it might be useful to them too.

It doesn't need to be long. A few honest lines are more than enough.

Thanks for reading, and for taking the time to be here.

www.ingramcontent.com/pod-product-compliance
Lightning Source LLC
Chambersburg PA
CBHW060505080526
44584CB00015B/1557